I Share My Ideas.
I Am BOLD!

My Amazing Toddler Behavioral Series

An Affirmation-Themed Book For Toddlers About Being Bold (Ages 2-4)

By

Suzanne T. Christian

TWORAVENS
B O O K S

Two Little Ravens
CHILDREN'S NON-FICTION BOOKS

Paperback Edition: 9781964202266
Hardcover Edition: 9781964202273
Digital Edition: 9781964202280

Published in the United States by Two Ravens Books LLC,
254 Chapman Rd, Ste 209, Newark DE 19702

'Expand the mind, free the imagination, one title at a time.'
www.tworavensbooks.com

Welcome to
"I Share My Ideas. I Am Bold!"

This book is a delightful collection of easy-to-understand affirmations designed specifically for young children. As you explore its pages together, your child will learn the importance of confidence, courage, and self-expression.

Each page features vibrant illustrations and relatable scenarios encouraging bold and adventurous interactions. By making this book a regular part of your reading routine, you can witness a gradual boost in your toddler's confidence, as repetition is a proven teaching tool.

Prepare for a journey of personal growth, courage, and lots of fun with your toddler!

I am unique.
I am **BOLD!**

I say "Hello" to make new friends.
I am **BOLD!**

I ask questions
when I'm curious.

I say
"Help, please"
when I need it.

I paint with bright colors all by myself.

Giant slides are fun—
I can do it!

Trying new foods is
a tasty adventure!

New games are exciting to learn.

I sing my favorite
song out loud.
I am bold!

I dance when I hear music playing.

At the dentist,
I open wide.
I am Bold!

When the nurse measures me.
I stand still.

I sit still at the doctor.
Ba-Bump, Ba-Bump!
I am **BOLD!**

I am **BOLD!**
Just like a superhero.

Meeting new friends is fun.
I am BOLD!

I share my stories with my friends.

The barber snips my hair.
Snip, Snip!
I am brave!

I giggle when I try something silly and new. I am bold!

Every day, I try something new.

I share my ideas.
I Am BOLD!
The End!

My Amazing Toddler Behavioral Series

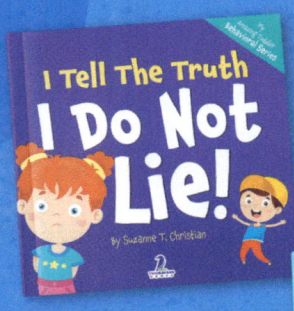
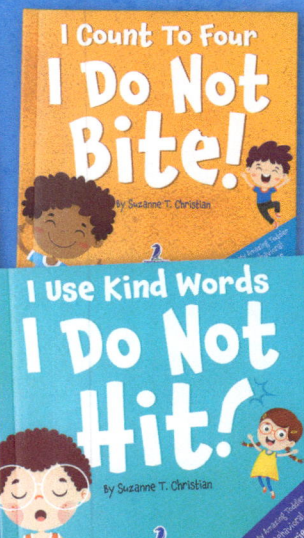
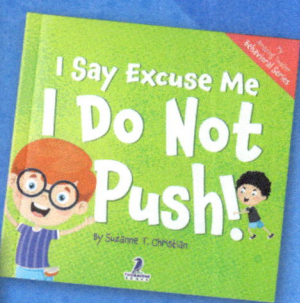

Check Out
Suzanne T. Christian's beloved series
'My Amazing Toddler Behavioral Series'.
Young readers are sure to enjoy!

Two Little Ravens
CHILDREN'S NON-FICTION BOOKS

Dear Amazing Reader,

Thank you for diving into **I Share My Ideas. I Am Bold!** with me. If this book touched your heart or made a difference for a young reader, I'd be grateful if you could share your thoughts in a review. Your feedback inspires my future work and helps others discover the magic within these pages.

I'd love to hear from you directly if you have suggestions or ideas for improving the book. Please feel free to reach out to me at suzanne.christian@tworavensbooks.com. Your voice counts, and I cherish it deeply.

With heartfelt gratitude,